TUSCANY STYLE

TUSCANY

Landscapes, Terraces & Houses

Interiors Details
STYLE

EDITOR
Angelika Taschen

TASCHEN

HONG KONG KÖLN LONDON LOS ANGELES MADRID PARIS TOKYO

To stay informed about upcoming TASCHEN titles, please request our magazine
at www.taschen.com/magazine or write to TASCHEN, Hohenzollernring 53,
D–50672 Cologne, Germany, contact@taschen.com, Fax: +49-221-254919.
We will be happy to send you a free copy of our magazine which is filled with
information about all of our books.

Original edition: © 2003 TASCHEN GmbH
Concept and Layout by Angelika Taschen, Cologne
Cover design by Angelika Taschen, Claudia Frey, Cologne
Project Management by Stephanie Bischoff, Cologne
Texts by Christiane Reiter, Berlin
Lithography by Horst Neuzner, Cologne
English Translation by Klaus Ziegler, Cologne
French Translation by Anne Charrière, Cologne

Printed in China
ISBN 978–3–8365–0765–3

CONTENTS SOMMAIRE INHALT

Italy – so often a place where we would rather be. With its towns and cities whose art treasures no auctioneer could possibly appraise; with its landscapes that seem to have been made specially for a soft-focus lens; with its light breezes from the sea, the smell of pine wood and fresh coffee in the air. And if you encounter all of these charms in the same spot and at the same time, you cannot possibly be anywhere else but in Tuscany. Situated in a seemingly unspectacular part of Italy's boot, Tuscany is a region which embodies the magic of the entire country within its 23,000 square kilometres. The cathedral of Florence, Siena's Piazza del Campo and the Leaning Tower of Pisa are pictures that immediately appear in our mind's eye, even if we have never been there ourselves. Less sharp, perhaps, are our mental images of Lucca, Volterra or Greve in Chianti; but the impressions that such dreams leave with us are the same. Admittedly, Tuscany has its kitsch and its clichés, its schmaltzy, sentimental violins, but it has another side, too, and one which could not be further removed, for it is precisely from Tuscany's centuries-old history that a modern paradise has emerged. The region offers everything the traveller in our new millennium could possibly

IN THE LAND OF THE CYPRESSES

Christiane Reiter

L'Italie – ce lieu où si souvent nous souhaiterions être. Avec des sites artistiques qu'aucun commissaire-priseur ne saurait apprécier à sa juste valeur, des paysages pour lesquels la photographie inventa l'image adoucie, et dans l'air, un soupçon de parfum de mer, de pin et de café. S'il est un lieu qui concentre cette nostalgie, c'est bien la Toscane. Cette région apparemment sans prétention, qui longe la tige de la botte, réunit pourtant sur 23 000 kilomètres carrés la magie de tout un pays. La cathédrale de Florence, la Piazza del Campo de Sienne et la tour penchée de Pise font partie des images gravées en chacun de nous – même si nous n'y avons encore jamais été. Un flou un peu plus grand estompe notre vision de Lucca, de Volterra ou de Greve, dans le Chianti; mais l'impression de vie que de tels rêves nous laissent demeure la même. Certes, par certains côtés, on frôle le kitsch et les accords de violon sirupeux, mais on en est aussi aux antipodes. De ses racines anciennes, la Toscane a tiré un paradis moderne, offrant tout ce que des voyageurs du troisième millénaire peuvent désirer, sans rien

Italien – das ist so oft der Ort, an dem wir lieber wären. Mit Kunststädten, deren Wert kein Auktionator schätzen kann, Landschaften, für die der Weichzeichner erfunden wurde und einem Hauch von Meer, Pinien und Kaffee in der Luft. Und wenn es ein Konzentrat dieser Sehnsucht gibt, dann ist es die Toskana. Eine Region, die scheinbar unspektakulär am Schaft des Stiefels liegt und doch auf 23 000 Quadratkilometern den Zauber eines ganzen Landes birgt. Der Dom von Florenz, Sienas Piazza del Campo und der Schiefe Turm von Pisa gehören zu den Bildern, die jeder jederzeit im Kopf hat – selbst wenn er noch nie dort war. Etwas mehr Unschärfe liegt über Szenen aus Lucca, Volterra oder Greve in Chianti; aber das Lebensgefühl, das solche Träume hinterlassen, bleibt dasselbe. Zugegeben: Es klingt nach Kitsch, Klischee und schmelzenden Geigen – und ist zugleich Welten davon entfernt. Die Toskana hat aus ihren alten Wurzeln ein modernes Paradies gezogen, sie bietet alles, was sich Reisende im dritten Jahrtausend wünschen und vergisst dabei nichts, was in den vergangenen Epochen

desire, but without once losing sight of its past. Not only such great and mighty families as the Medici have left their mark on the towns and countryside of Tuscany, but the simple country folk, too. The Tuscans have never kept themselves to themselves, for Tuscany has always needed strangers, just as strangers have always needed Tuscany. Tuscany's atmosphere is unique, and so is its style. It is a style that has inspired designers all over the world, though none of them has ever quite succeeded in matching it. Now-here else in the world do terracotta-tiled floors gleam with such warmth. Nowhere else in the world does linen hang and fold with such fortuitous perfection. Nowhere else in the world does wood exude such sweet fragrance. Let yourself be captivated by the light and colours of Tuscany; dream of the simple luxury and luxurious simplicity of its style, of its culture and its cuisine. And if on this or that photograph you can make out a rotting window sill, a loose tile or an olive twig that peeks cheekily into the picture, you will have recognized one of those loveable shortcomings that lend Tuscany its charm and make it so relaxing, so hospitable and so – to put it in a nutshell – perfect.

oublier des époques passées. Villes et campagnes ont été conçues avec art et artifice, par des clans puissants comme celui des Médicis, mais aussi par de simples paysans. Tout ce monde ne s'est jamais renfermé sur lui-même, car en Toscane on a besoin des étrangers, comme les étrangers ont besoin de la Toscane. L'atmosphère et le style caractéristiques de la Toscane inspirent les créateurs du monde entier, sans jamais être totalement égalés. Nulle part ailleurs, les sols en terre cuite ne brillent d'une lumière aussi chaude qu'ici, nulle part la toile de lin est drapée avec autant de précision désinvolte, nulle part le bois n'exhale cette intense et douce odeur. Laissez-vous captiver par la lumière et les couleurs de la Toscane, rêvez de luxe et de simplicité, de culture et de gastronomie. Et si vous découvrez sur l'une ou l'autre photo une planche vermoulue, un carreau de faïence décollé ou une branche d'olivier qui s'impose effrontément dans l'image, vous avez repéré une des petites irrégularités qui rendent la Toscane si charmante, si chaleureuse, si sereine – en un mot, si parfaite.

geschehen ist. Stadt und Land sind hier künstlich und kunstvoll geschaffen worden, von mächtigen Clans wie den Medici, aber auch von einfachen Bauern. All diese Menschen sind dabei nie unter sich geblieben, denn in der Toskana braucht man die Fremden, wie die Fremden die Toskana brauchen. Wie die Atmosphäre, so ist auch der Stil der Toskana einzigartig, inspiriert Designer in aller Welt und wird doch niemals ganz erreicht. Die Terrakottaböden leuchten eben nirgendwo sonst so warm wie hier, das Leinen wird nirgendwo sonst so zufällig-exakt drapiert, das Holz verströmt nirgendwo sonst diesen zart-intensiven Duft. Lassen Sie sich vom Licht und den Farben der Toskana einfangen, träumen Sie vom Einfachen und doch Luxuriösen, von Kultur und Kulinarik. Und wenn Sie auf der ein oder anderen Aufnahme ein morsches Brett entdecken, eine lose Kachel oder einen Olivenzweig, der vorwitzig ins Bild ragt, haben Sie eine der kleinen Unzulänglich-keiten erkannt, die die Toskana erst so charmant, warmherzig und gelassen machen, wie sie ist – mit einem Wort: perfekt.

"…Fields, hedges and cypresses embellished by a corona of light, reminding one of the golden waves running over the grass in the foreground of Botticelli's 'Birth of Venus'…"

Edith Wharton (1905)

«…Champs, haies et cyprès étaient enveloppés d'une auréole de lumière rappelant les ondes dorées déferlant sur l'herbe au premier plan de la ‹Naissance de Vénus› de Boticelli…»

Edith Wharton (1905)

»…Felder, Hecken und Zypressen waren von von einer Lichtaureole umhüllt, die an die goldenen Wellen denken ließ, die im Vordergrund von Botticellis Geburt der Venus‹ über das Gras laufen…«

Edith Wharton (1905)

LANDSCAPES
TERRACES & HOUSES

Paysages, Terrasses & Maisons
Landschaften, Terrassen & Häuser

10/11 The vineyard near at hand: The Castello di Gabbiano. *La vigne devant la porte : le Castello di Gabbiano.* Den Weinberg vor der Tür: Das Castello di Gabbiano.
Photo: Eric Laignel & Patricia Parinejad

12/13 A lady made of stone: Wanda Ferragamo's house. *Une dame de pierre : dans la propriété de Wanda Ferragamos.* Eine Dame aus Stein: Auf Wanda Ferragamos Anwesen.
Photo: Reto Guntli

14/15 Cypress Skyline: Garden of the architect P. Castellini. *Horizon de cyprès : dans le jardin de l'architecte P. Castellini.* Skyline aus Zypressen: Im Garten des Architekten P. Castellini.
Photo: Guy Bouchet/Inside

16/17 Diving in happiness: Roberto Budini-Gattai's swimming pool. *Plonger dans le bonheur : la piscine de Roberto Budini-Gattai.* Kopfüber ins Glück: Der Pool von Roberto Budini-Gattai.

18/19 Behind mighty doors: The villa di Tizzano. *Derrière d'imposantes portes : la villa di Tizzano.* Hinter mächtigen Toren: Die Villa di Tizzano.

20/21 It's all symmetry: A garden in Colli Fiorentini. *Tout est symétrie : un jardin dans les Colli fiorentini.* Alles ist Symmetrie: Ein Garten in den Colli fiorentini.

22/23 Kept in style: View of the vineyards. *Un soin exemplaire : les vignes.* Musterhaft gepflegt: In den Weinbergen.
Photo: Gianni Berengo Gardin

24/25 In the sun: Leisa and Michael Snyder's house. *Dans la lumière : la maison de Leisa et de Michael Snyder.* Im Licht: Das Haus von Leisa und Michael Snyder.
Photo: Karsten Damstedt

26/27 Light and shade: In front of Wolfgang Storch's house. *Ombre et soleil : devant la propriété de Wolfgang Storch.* Sonne und Schatten: Vor Wolfgang Storchs Besitz.
Photo: Eric Laignel & Patricia Parinejad

28/29 A beautiful espalier: Gateway up to the hills. *Bel espalier : la porte des collines.* Schönes Spalier: Das Tor zu den Hügeln.
Photo: Eric Laignel & Patricia Parinejad

30/31 Monica Sangberg Moen and Stefano Crivelli's vantage point. *Point de vue chez Monica Sangberg Moen et Stefano Crivelli.* Aussichtsplatz von Monica Sangberg Moen und Stefano Crivelli.
Photo: Eric Laignel & Patricia Parinejad

32/33 A place in the sun: Tuscany invites you to take a seat. *A la lumière du soleil : la Toscane invite à déjeuner.* Im Sonnenschein: Die Toskana bittet zu Tisch.
Photo: Eric Laignel & Patricia Parinejad

34/35 The smell of summer: Herbs and spices, freshly picked. *Les senteurs de l'été : herbes et épices, fraîchement cueillies.* So duftet der Sommer: Kräuter und Gewürze, frisch gepflückt. *Photo: Bärbel Miebach*

36/37 Open house: Arturo Carmassi's villa. *Des portes toujours ouvertes : la villa d'Arturo Carmassi.* Wo die Türen immer offen stehen: Arturo Carmassis Villa. *Photo: Mads Morgensen*

38/39 Endless avenues: A walk beneath cypresses. *Des allées sans fin : promenade sous les cyprès.* Endlose Alleen: Ein Spaziergang unter Zypressen. *Photo: Mads Morgensen*

40/41 In full bloom: Carmassi's garden at dawn. *En pleine floraison : le jardin de Carmassi au crépuscule.* In voller Blüte: Carmassis Garten in der Dämmerung. *Photo: Mads Morgensen*

42/43 As though calculated: Way up to Marilena and Lorenzo Bonomo. *Tracé à la perfection : le chemin vers Marilena et Lorenzo Bonomo.* Wie abgezirkelt: Der Weg zu Marilena und Lorenzo Bonomo.

44/45 Green as far as the horizon: The most beautiful views of Tuscany. *Vert jusqu'à l'horizon : les plus beaux aspects de la Toscane.* Grün bis zum Horizont: Die schönsten Seiten der Toskana.

46/47 Geometry: In front of the villa le Carceri. *Notes rondes : devant la villa le Carceri.* Eine runde Sache: Vor der Villa le Carceri.

48/49 In Mediterranean colours: House of the architect P. Castellini. *Dans les couleurs du Sud : la maison de l'architecte P. Castellini.* In südlichen Farben: Das Haus des Architekten P. Castellini. *Photo: Guy Bouchet/Inside*

50/51 Resting place under arches: Siesta in Patio. *Repos sous les arcades : la sieste dans le Patio.* Ruheplatz unter Bögen: Siesta im Patio. *Photo: Guy Bouchet/Inside*

52/53 Dinner table for friends: In Maremma. *Table de fête pour les amis : dans la Maremma.* Festtafel für Freunde: In der Maremma.

54/55 A turquoise dream: Pool of the villa La Querciola. *Un rêve couleur turquoise : la piscine de la villa La Querciola.* Ein Traum in Türkis: Der Pool der Villa La Querciola. *Photo: Andreas von Einsiedel*

56/57 Summerhouse with a view: In front of Simone de Looze's house. *Tonnelle et point de vue : devant la maison de Simone de Looze.* Laube mit Aussicht: Vor dem Haus von Simone de Looze. *Photo: Mirjam Bleeker/Taverne Agency*

58/59 Nothing but nature: Relaxation for body and soul. *Tout autour rien que la nature : détente pour le corps et l'âme.* Ringsum nichts als Natur: Entspannung für Körper und Seele. *Photo: Mirjam Bleeker/Taverne Agency*

60/61 Keep things rolling: Playing boules in Tuscany. *Ça roule : jeu de boule en Toscane.* Die Kugel rollt: Boule in der Toskana. *Photo: Mirjam Bleeker/Taverne Agency*

62/63 Perfect swing: Sport Italian style. *Elan parfait : sport à l'italienne.* Perfekter Schwung: Sportstunde auf Italienisch. *Photo: Mirjam Bleeker/Taverne Agency*

64/65 All in red: Poppy in bloom. *Tout en rouge : le coquelicot en fleur.* Ganz in Rot: Der Klatschmohn blüht. *Photo: Mirjam Bleeker/Taverne Agency*

66/67 Green garage: Even the cars take a holiday. *Garage vert : même les voitures sont en vacances.* Grüne Garage: Selbst die Autos machen Urlaub.
Photo: Mirjam Bleeker/Taverne Agency

68/69 Steps to the siesta: At Simone de Looze house. *Marches vers la sieste : dans la maison de Simone de Looze.* Die Stufen zur Siesta: Das Haus von Simone de Looze.
Photo: Mirjam Bleeker/Taverne Agency

70/71 Keeping cool: Shady place under the large awning. *Vaste espace : à l'ombre sous la grande marquise.* Auf voller Länge: Schatten-plätze unter der großen Markise.
Photo: Mirjam Bleeker/Taverne Agency

72/73 Tree of life: In front of Brigitte Erm's villa. *Arbre de vie : devant la villa de Brigitte Erm.* Baum des Lebens: Vor der Villa von Brigitte Erm.
Photo: Pep Escoda

74/75 Olive grove of one's own: A house in Maremma. *Avec son oliveraie personnelle : une maison dans la Maremma.* Mit eigenem Olivenhain: Ein Haus in der Maremma.

76/77 Country style cuisine: In front of the villa Montosoli. *Cuisine campagnarde par excellence : devant la villa Montosoli.* Land-hausküche pur: Vor der Villa Montosoli.

"...The light fell on marble walls; then on marble floor, interspersed with other stones. Mattresses were put out to air; the house exuded the feeling of summery slumbering abandonment..."

Alfred Kerr in: Du bist so schön! Die Welt im Licht II (1920)

« ...La lumière tombait sur les murs de marbre, puis sur le sol de marbre parsemé d'autres pierres. Les matelas avaient été exposés à l'air; tout dans la maison dégageait une impression de somnolence estivale... »

Alfred Kerr dans: Du bist so schön! Die Welt im Licht II (1920)

» ...Das Licht fiel auf Marmorwände; dann auf marmornen Boden, mit andrem Gestein durchsetzt. Matratzen lagen zum Lüften gebreitet; alles in dem Haus ver-strömte das Gefühl sommerlich schlummernder Verlassenheit...«

Alfred Kerr in: Du bist so schön! Die Welt im Licht II (1920)

INTERIORS

Intérieurs   Interieurs

84/85 Leaning back: A glass of wine on the veranda. *Confortablement assis : un verre de vin sur la véranda.* Bequem zurückgelehnt: Ein Glas Wein auf der Veranda.
Photo: Andreas von Einsiedel

86/87 The colour of mauve: Room in Mediterranean style. *La couleur mauve : refuge dans le style du sud.* Die Farbe Lila: Refugium im Stil des Südens.
Photo: Andreas von Einsiedel

88/89 View of the bed: Inside Monica Sangberg Moen and Stefano Crivelli's house. *Coup d'œil sur le lit : dans la maison de Monica Sangberg Moen et Stefano Crivelli.* Blick ins Bett: Im Haus von Monica Sangberg Moen und Stefano Crivelli.
Photo: Eric Laignel & Patricia Parinejad

90/91 Splashes of green: As fresh as nature itself. *Nuances de vert : frais comme la nature.* Akzente in Grün: So frisch wie die Natur selbst.
Photo: Eric Laignel & Patricia Parinejad

92/93 Spacious: Tenuta di Trinoro's kitchen. *Joli cadre : la cuisine de Tenuta di Trinoro.* Schöner Rahmen: Tenuta di Trinoros Küche.

94/95 Handpainted: This bed promises blue dreams. *Peint à la main : un lit à rêver en bleu.* Handbemalt: Ein Bett verspricht blaue Träume.

96/97 Under the sign of the olive: Le Belvedere's kitchen. *Sous le signe de l'olive : la cuisine du Belvedere.* Im Zeichen der Olive: Die Küche von Le Belvedere.

98/99 Abundant with delicacies: Invitation by Leisa und Michael Snyder. *Table riche : Leisa et Michael Snyder invitent.* Reich gedeckt: Leisa und Michael Snyder laden ein.
Photo: Karsten Damstedt

100/101 As if on stage: Inside the villa Roncioni. *Comme une scène de théâtre : dans la villa Roncioni.* Wie eine Theaterbühne: In der Villa Roncioni.
Photo: Massimo Listri

102/103 True to original: Mural painting in trompe-l'oeil style. *Fidèle à l'original : peintures murales à la manière des trompe-l'œil.* Originalgetreu: Wandmalereien nach Trompe-l'oeil- Art.
Photo: Massimo Listri

104/105 Frugal and classy: Inside Cesare Rovatti's house. *Sobre et élégant : dans la maison de Cesare Rovatti.* Schlicht und elegant: Im Haus von Cesare Rovatti.

106/107 Mixed styles: P. Castellini's living room. *Mélange de styles : le séjour de P. Castellini.* Stilmix: Das Wohnzimmer von P. Castellini.
Photo: Guy Bouchet/Inside

108/109 Dual function: Both wardrobe and treasure chest. *Double usage : à la fois armoire et coffre à trésors.* Doppelt genutzt: Schrank und Schatztruhe zugleich.
Photo: Guy Bouchet/Inside

110/111 Pure relaxation: A night in a four-poster bed. *Détente à l'état pur : une nuit dans un lit à baldaquin.* Entspannung pur: Eine Nacht im Himmelbett.
Photo: Guy Bouchet/Inside

112/113 Under old rafters: Reading room with open hearth. *Sous de vieilles poutres : chambre de lecture avec cheminée ouverte.* Unter alten Balken: Lesezimmer mit offenem Kamin.
Photo: Eric Laignel & Patricia Parinejad

114/115 All aglow: Dinner by the fireside. *Tout en rouge : un dîner au coin du feu.* Ganz in Rot: Ein Abendessen am Kamin.
Photo: Eric Laignel & Patricia Parinejad

116/117 Spick and span: Inside the villa Le Carceri. *Astiquée à fond : la villa Le Carceri.* Blitzblank poliert: In der Villa Le Carceri.

118/119 Back to the past: The kitchen of the villa Belsedere. *Regard vers le passé : la cuisine de la villa Belsedere.* Blick in die Vergangenheit: Die Küche der Villa Belsedere.

120/121 Pink table decoration: Nature indoors. *Décor de table rose : la nature pénètre directement dans la maison.* Tischschmuck in Pink: Die Natur kommt direkt ins Haus.

122/123 Behind thick walls: Living like Simone de Looze. *Derrière de gros murs : habiter comme Simone de Looze.* Hinter dicken Mauern: Wohnen wie Simone de Looze. *Photo: Mirjam Bleeker/Taverne Agency*

124/125 Checkered and striped: Effective simple patterns. *Carreaux et rayures : des motifs simples qui font de l'effet.* Karriert und gestreift: Einfach-effektive Muster. *Photo: Mirjam Bleeker/Taverne Agency*

126/127 Well covered: One of Simone de Looze's bedrooms. *Bien couvert : dans une chambre à coucher de Simone de Looze.* Gut zugedeckt: In einem Schlafzimmer von Simone de Looze. *Photo: Mirjam Bleeker/Taverne Agency*

128/129 Sources of light: Sunbeams shining
through windows and doors. *Sources de
lumière : des rayons de soleil dansent à travers
portes et fenêtres.* Lichtquellen: Durch Fenster
und Tür tanzen Sonnenstrahlen.
Photo: Mirjam Bleeker/Taverne Agency

130/131 Tidy: A plain wall unit in the room.
*Soigneusement rangé : chambre avec éléments
de rangement muraux.* Sauber aufgeräumt:
Zimmer mit schlichter Schrankwand.
Photo: Mirjam Bleeker/Taverne Agency

132/133 Refreshing: Shower with a view of
the garden. *L'élément eau : douche avec vue
sur le jardin.* Im nassen Element: Dusche mit
Blick in den Garten.
Photo: Mirjam Bleeker/Taverne Agency

134/135 Spacious: Simone de Looze await
her guests. *Beaucoup de place : Simone de
Looze attend ses invités.* Viel Platz: Simone de
Looze wartet auf Gäste.
Photo: Mirjam Bleeker/Taverne Agency

136/137 Venerable walls: Where cooking is
a great experience. *Murs vénérables : quand
la cuisine devient événement.* Ehrwürdige
Mauern: Hier wird Kochen zum Erlebnis.
Photo: Mirjam Bleeker/Taverne Agency

"…The outside wall of my room is covered with yellow, ripely smelling roses and small yellow flowers, not unlike to dogroses; just growing a bit more quietly and more obediently up the high trellis…"

Rainer Maria Rilke in: Das Florenzer Tagebuch (1898)

« …Le mur extérieur de ma chambre est recouvert de roses jaunes au parfum musqué et de petites fleurs jaunes qui ne sont pas sans rappeler l'églantine sauvage ; elles ne se font qu'un peu plus silencieuses et plus obéissantes en grimpant le long des hauts espaliers… »

Rainer Maria Rilke dans: Das Florenzer Tagebuch (1898)

» …Die Wand meines Zimmers ist nach außen hin mit gelben, reif duftenden Rosen und kleinen gelben Blumen überblüht, die wilden Heckenröschen nicht unähnlich sind; sie steigen nur etwas stiller und gehorsamer die hohen Spaliere hinauf…«

Rainer Maria Rilke in: Das Florenzer Tagebuch (1898)

DETAILS

Détails Details

A MARIA SS. DELLA [...]
PROTEGGITRICE DI [...]
ED A S. VINCENZO [...]
QUESTO SACELLO
CON MISTICHE CERIMONIE [...]
IL DI 22 SETTEMBRE [...]
DA MONS. GIUSEPPE TO[...]
VESCOVO DI VOLTER[...]
I FRATELLI TOMAS[...]
[...]

MON MONDE
C'EST moN
DeMoN MoN
MoNdE C'EsT
mOn DeMoN

1000

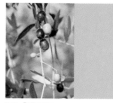

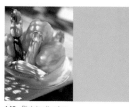

144 Delicacies:
Freshly picked olives.
*Un délice: olives
fraîchement cueillies.*
Köstlichkeiten: Oliven,
frisch vom Baum.
*Photo: Eric Laignel &
Patricia Parinejad*

146 Stoneware:
Crockery in Tuscan
colours. *Grès : vais-
selle aux couleurs de
la Toscane.* Steingut:
Geschirr in den Far-
ben der Toskana.
*Photo: Eric Laignel &
Patricia Parinejad*

147 Two-coloured:
Black and green
olives. *Bicolore :
olives noires et vertes.*
Zweifarbig: Schwarze
und grüne Oliven.
*Photo: Eric Laignel &
Patricia Parinejad*

148 Rich in vitamins:
Zucchinis and paprika.
*Riches en vitamines :
courgettes et poivrons.*
Vitaminreich: Zucchini
und Paprika.
*Photo:
Karsten Damstedt*

150 Ripe: Dark purple
grapes. *Certificat de
maturité : raisins noirs.*
Reifezeugnis: Blaue
Weintrauben.

151 Proud: Statue
of a cock. *Gonflée
d'orgueil : une statue
de coq.* Stolz ge-
schwellt: Eine Hahnen-
statue.

153 Delicacies: Ham,
cheese and bread.
*Les délices du palais :
jambon, fromage et
pain.* Delikatessen:
Schinken, Käse und
Brot.

154 In rows: Home-
made sauce. *En
rangées : la sauce
maison.* Aufgereiht:
Hausgemachte Sauce.

155 Ripened by the
sun: Tuscan tomatoes.
*Mûries au so-leil :
tomates de Toscane.*
Sonnengereift: Tos-
kanische Tomaten.

156 Needlework:
Filigree embroidery.
*Fait main : broderie de
filigrane.* Handarbeit:
Filigrane Stickerei.

158 Memory:
Engraved in stone.
*Souvenir : écriture
dans la pierre.*
Erinnerung: Schrift
in Stein.
*Photo: Eric Laignel &
Patricia Parinejad*

159 Framed: Portrait
of a monk. *Encadré :
portrait d'un moine.*
Eingerahmt: Portrait
eines Mönchs.

161 Heraldic ani-
mal: Printed on cloth.
*Animal de blason :
imprimé sur tissu.*
Wappentier: Auf Stoff
gedruckt.

162 A matter of faith: Antique wall decoration. *Affaire de croyance : décoration murale antique.* Glaubenssache: Antiker Wandschmuck.

163 Picture gallery: Individual souvernirs. *Galerie de tableaux : souvenirs personnels.* Bildergalerie: Persönliche Souvenirs.

165 Play of Colours: Crockery cupboard. *Jeux de couleur : vaisselier à l'ancienne.* Farbenspiel: Neuer alter Geschirrschrank. *Photo: Andreas von Einsiedel*

166 In pairs: Shoes in the entrance hall. *Par deux : collection de chaussures dans l'entrée.* Paarweise: Schuhsammlung im Flur.

169 Silver sheen: Olive twig on linen. *Eclat argenté : branche d'oliver sur lin.* Silberglanz: Olivenzweig auf Leinen. *Photo: Eric Laignel & Patricia Parinejad*

170 Refreshing: Antique stone basin. *Rafraîchissant : bac ancien en pierre.* Erfrischung: Antikes Steinbecken.

171 Noble: sumptuously ornate bathroom. *Point d'eau : une salle de bain richement décorée.* Wasserstelle: Reich verziertes Bad.

173 Turning points: Polished taps. *Invitation à tourner : des ferrures bien polies.* Drehmomente: Polierte Armaturen. *Photo: Mirjam Bleeker/ Taverne Agency*

174 Treasures of the sea: Twisted shells. *Trésors marins : coquillage vrillés.* Meeresschätze: Gedrehte Muscheln. *Photo: Mirjam Bleeker/ Taverne Agency*

175 From the woods: Freshly picked mushrooms. *Messagers de la fo-rêt: champignons fraîchement cueillis.* Waldboten: Frisch gepflückte Pilze. *Photo: Mirjam Bleeker/ Taverne Agency*

177 Accessory: A heavy wine cooler. *Au frais sur la table : un pot qui pèse son poids.* Tischaccessoire: Schwerer Weinkühler. *Photo: Mirjam Bleeker/ Taverne Agency*

178 Fruit bowl: Juicy melons. *As-siette de fruits : melons juteux.* Obstteller: Saftige Melonen. *Photo: Mirjam Bleeker/ Taverne Agency*

179 Just harvested: Chilli and paprika. *Tout juste récoltés : piments et poivrons.* Erntefrisch: Peperoni und Paprika. *Photo: Mirjam Bleeker/ Taverne Agency*

181 Spicy: Fresh
garlic. *Assaisonne-*
ment : ail frais.
Gewürz: Frischer
Knoblauch.
Photo:
Mirjam Bleeker/
Taverne Agency

182 Flourishing:
View of the garden.
Floraison : regard sur
le jardin. Aufgeblüht:
Blick in den Garten.
Photo:
Mirjam Bleeker/
Taverne Agency

183 Like pearls:
Coloured boules.
Comme des perles :
boules multicolores.
Perlengleich: Bunte
Boulekugeln.
Photo:
Mirjam Bleeker/
Taverne Agency

184 Withdrawn:
Curtains made of
fine cloth. *Intimité :*
rideaux d'étoffes
délicates. Zurück-
gezogen: Gardinen
aus zartem Stoff.

186 Artworks:
Fabrics embroidered
with loving care.
Œuvres d'art : tissus
brodés avec amour.
Kunstwerke: Liebevoll
bestickte Stoffe.
Photo: Eric Laignel &
Patricia Parinejad

187 Natural:
Flowers in a blue
glass. *Naturel : fleurs*
dans un verre bleu.
Natürlich: Blumen in
blauem Glas.
Photo:
Simon Mc Bride/
Franca Speranza